IN YOUR FEELS

A JOURNAL TO EXPLORE YOUR EMOTIONS

EMILY EDLYNN, PHD
FOREWORD BY MARISA LASCALA
SENIOR PARENTING EDITOR, GOOD HOUSEKEEPING

kids
HEARST
HOME

CONTENTS

FOREWORD

Emotions are so important. They make us who we are. They influence how we behave, and they affect our relationships with the people around us. And the only way to truly understand our emotions—the highs and the lows and the in-between feelings—is to spend some time with them and figure out what triggers them.

That's the purpose of this journal: to truly understand your feelings—what they are, how they work, and how they make us react to others. Paying attention to your feelings might be tricky at first, but if you slow down, tune in, and really examine them, you will gain a deeper understanding of yourself.

The important thing is to be totally honest with yourself, and this journal is a safe place to express exactly how you feel. It's for your eyes only. (To any adults, siblings, or friends peeking inside: *Close this book now and have some respect for privacy!*) And if this journal makes you realize there are things you want to share with your friends or the grown-ups in your life, there are many ideas for how to talk about them. But this space? It's just for you.

MARISA LASCALA,
Senior parenting editor at Good Housekeeping

PSST... This isn't a regular book, so you don't have to go in order! Skip around to the emotions and activities that best fit your feels for the day.

BEING IN YOUR FEELS

Have you ever watched a sports game and seen an athlete get really angry after a play? Maybe you have a younger sibling who bursts into tears whenever they don't get their way. Or do you know a friend or classmate who seems super calm until — **BAM!** — they explode? These are all examples of being *in your feels*.

Think about how *you* feel your feelings: do they feel like towering ocean waves, or more like calm ripples that gently brush the shore? What do you do with these feelings? Do you try hard to keep them stuffed inside? Or do you put it all out there by shouting and slamming doors when you're upset, or by cheering and dancing when you're happy?

Letting yourself be *in your feels* — no matter how uncomfortable they might be — is really OK, totally normal, and even good for you! But how you act on your feelings makes a difference. If you're angry and you blow up at your friend, they probably don't want to be around you and then you're even more upset! But keeping anger inside could make you more likely to explode. If you can talk about it with a good friend, this helps you get support and feel better.

This journal gives you a space to get to know you and your feelings. You will learn about why all humans have emotions and how they connect with your thoughts, body, and actions. Then, through dozens of fun activities, you'll explore the most common feelings and discover some awesome ideas to help you handle them like a pro.

INTRODUCTION
HOW FEELINGS WORK

HOW DO YOU FEEL RIGHT NOW?

Maybe you said "great" or "meh" or even "I'm not sure." Now add these questions: How does your body feel (tense, relaxed, in pain)? What are your thoughts? ("I feel good, but I'm not sure why," or "I'm having a bad day.") What are you doing? (Maybe biting your nails or lying down comfortably on the couch.)

Feelings are made up of the different ways you react to something that happens: what you're thinking, how your body feels, and what you do. In this book, you'll explore all those reactions to help you more confidently answer the question: *How do I really feel?*

Knowing how you feel day to day and moment to moment — including which emotions are part of that feeling — is a huge part of understanding yourself. Life can be full of challenges, from fights with friends to confusing homework assignments to feeling that your parents just don't understand you. But the more you take time to get to know your emotions and how to cope with them, the more confident you will feel about taking on life's challenges — and the more you can enjoy the fun things in life.

To help us explore feelings and what triggers them, let's start with something *everyone* deals with: **STRESS**.

STRESSED OUT OR STRESS SWEET SPOT?

You've probably heard people say "I'm sooooo stressed out!" But what exactly does that mean? Stress is when you feel pressure—and it's a common trigger for many emotions. (We'll talk more about triggers on page 18.) Having too much stress can feel like you're not in control over what's happening to you or around you. It can cause unpleasant emotions (like worry, frustration, and anger) or unpleasant body sensations (like headaches, stomachaches, or restlessness) when trying to sleep.

But stress isn't always a bad thing: Sometimes a little pressure can be good! It can motivate you to practice your instrument before a recital or study hard for a math test so you ace it. This is the sweet spot of stress—just enough pressure to make you curious and interested to work toward a goal important to you. Too little stress can make you feel bored or lazy.

Turn the page to identify your stress triggers and whether they're in the stress sweet spot or truly stressing you out.

HERE ARE A FEW THINGS THAT MIGHT STRESS YOU OUT:

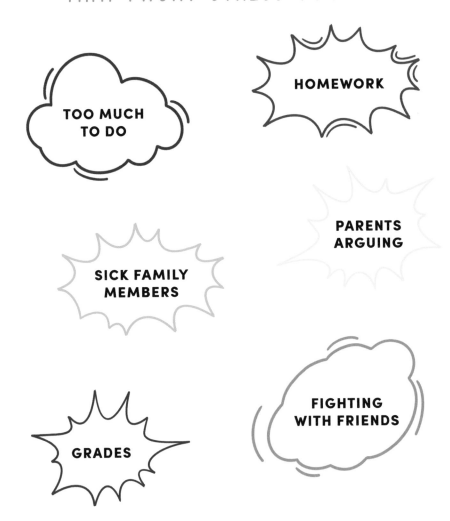

In the space on the next page, write down your stressors.

Put an X on the side where you think your stress triggers fall—
just a little pressure that you can handle (SWEET SPOT) or too
big and hard (STRESSED OUT)?

SWEET
SPOT

STRESSED
OUT

YOUR COPING TOOLBOX

Feeling too much stress—just like feeling too big emotions—is overwhelming. But the good news is that you can use coping skills to help you feel calmer and more in control of your feelings. Just like a toolbox has different tools for different jobs, it's important to have a variety of coping tools to choose from. That way, if one tool isn't working for you or the type of feelings you're dealing with, you can move on to another one.

Throughout this book, you'll notice this picture of a toolbox to alert you when you're practicing a coping tool. Most of the tools you'll practice fall into one of the categories to the right.

And sometimes, one coping tool might cover more than one of these categories. **LET'S TAKE A CLOSER LOOK AT EACH.**

IN YOUR HEAD COPING

Your thoughts are powerful. If you tell yourself that you're going to fail a math test, you're more likely to feel anxious and not do well. If you think instead, *I studied hard and will do my best*, you will feel calmer and more confident—and will probably do better! You can find ways to use your thought power for good with In Your Head coping tools on pages 32, 44, 59, 64, 100, 110, 122, and 134.

1.
IN YOUR HEAD

Tools that change
ways of thinking
about stress or
an emotion.

2.
IN YOUR BODY

Tools that help you
notice and relax
your body when you
feel stress or a
strong emotion.

3.
ACCEPTANCE

Tools that help you name
how you're feeling and
let you feel it instead
of getting rid of it.

4.
EXPRESSION

Tools that get your
feelings out, either
through talking, writing,
or showing emotions.

5.
CONNECTION

Tools that show you how
to find support from
other people to help
you feel better.

IN YOUR BODY COPING

Our mind and body are always communicating with each other, like a Snapchat streak that goes on forever. Learning to relax your body helps clear your mind to have more helpful thoughts, which calms your emotions too. Two main tools to do this are deep breathing and meditation.

The Power of the Deep Breath

If someone says "just breathe" to calm you down, it might feel like they don't understand how upset you are. It sounds impossible that something as simple as taking a deep breath could help, but it's true. Scientists have seen how a deep breath—one that starts down in your belly—tells your brain that your body can rest and feel safe. Whether you're worried, angry, or scared, taking several slow, deep breaths sends messages to the brain that calm the body and the mind. For more exercises involving deep breathing, see pages 60 and 76.

Meditation Magic

Have you heard of meditation? It's the practice of sitting still and quieting your thoughts. Scientists have studied how meditation helps the brain de-stress, which helps the rest of the body relax too. Scientists also found that kids who meditate have calmer reactions to big emotions. For a meditation exercise, see page 132.

ACCEPTANCE COPING

When you have a tough emotion wash over you, like embarrassment or guilt or sadness, do you ever try to run away from the feeling? It's common to avoid emotions by doing other things, like scrolling through your cell phone or refusing to talk about how you feel when a parent asks. Part of acceptance is doing the opposite: facing your emotions and feeling them instead of pushing them away.

Of course, acceptance is easy with pleasant emotions like happiness, joy, and excitement. But it's especially powerful to pay attention to less pleasant emotions like anger, sadness, and worry. Accepting an emotion can be as simple as noting it or saying in your head, *I'm feeling so angry right now.* Accepting tough emotions instead of ignoring them can help you get through difficult moments faster. For more exercises to practice acceptance, see pages 46 and 74.

EXPRESSION AND CONNECTION COPING

Have you ever made slime with too much glue and you can't get it off your hands? When we're stressed out and having painful thoughts and emotions, they can get stuck in our minds just like that slime. Getting the thoughts and emotions out of your head is a form of taking care of ourselves. It's as necessary as sleeping, eating, and exercise. It can even help with our stress and, in turn, help us not get sick as often. Expressing emotions in healthy ways includes talking with others, writing down what you're feeling, and even crying. When you express emotions to others, this is connection, so these two types of coping often happen together. For more examples of expression and connection coping, see pages 50, 88, and 90.

Talk It Out

Talking about how you feel helps you have stronger friendships and connect to people you love, like parents, grandparents, other important grown-ups, siblings, and anyone else close to you. It can feel uncomfortable at first, especially if you're not used to it. That's why it's important to pick people you really trust who are good listeners.

Write It Out

There are times you may not feel ready to talk—you may not even know what to say! Writing in a journal can help you figure out how you feel and get those feelings out even when you're not ready to share them with others.

Don't like writing? You don't even have to write full sentences or any words at all. You could use a journal to write quick phrases about what's going on and how you feel, or you could draw—or both! It's all about what feels best to you.

Cry It Out

Some people feel embarrassed if they cry in front of other people, but everyone cries! When you cry with people you love and trust, this can help them understand that you need their support to feel better.

Now it's time to figure out what's going on in your brain and body. That's where the FEELINGS PATHWAY on page 18 comes in. Turn the page to take a trip down the pathway.

OVERPOWERING EMOTIONS

Sometimes unpleasant emotions (like sadness and anger) can become so strong that it's hard to feel pleasant emotions (like happiness). If you've experienced this, the coping tools in this journal can help. But if you still feel sad or angry most of the time, reach out to a trusted adult and let them know you need help.

THE FEELINGS PATHWAY

Every day you experience a lot of feelings. You might feel excited in the morning, worried by lunch, disappointed after school, and grateful by dinner — or all those feelings could happen in a single hour!

Every feeling starts with the same thing: **A TRIGGER**.

Triggers can be big moments, such as getting a new pet, or small moments, like falling in gym class. Sometimes a trigger can start in your mind, such as a happy or sad memory. Whatever the trigger is, it sparks emotion and starts you on a journey on the **FEELINGS PATHWAY**.

Feelings are made up of four elements:

- **EMOTIONS**
- **THOUGHTS**
- **BODY SENSATIONS**
- **BEHAVIORS**

Combined, these elements create the experience of a feeling — and they all affect one another too. Depending on the type of trigger and your response, the order in which you visit these stops on the Feelings Pathway can vary — you can go in any direction, and even zigzag around the four stops — but they're always linked. Turn the page, and we'll show you how it works!

CONTROL CENTER

The brain has a control panel for our emotions called the limbic system. When we have certain emotions — such as angry, happy, proud, or sad — our brain lights up in different areas, and chemicals called hormones affect your overall mood and how the body feels (like tense or relaxed).

TRAVELING THE FEELINGS PATHWAY

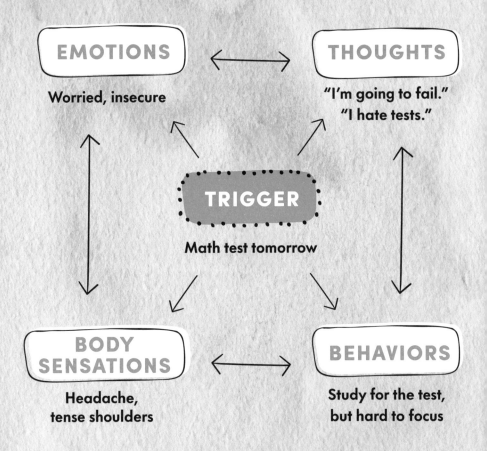

EMOTIONS

Worried, insecure

THOUGHTS

"I'm going to fail."
"I hate tests."

TRIGGER

Math test tomorrow

BODY SENSATIONS

Headache,
tense shoulders

BEHAVIORS

Study for the test,
but hard to focus

Body Sensations

Often the first stop on the Feelings Pathway, body sensations can signal to us that we need to check in with our emotions.

Emotions

Ask yourself, *How am I feeling right now?* The answer is the emotion you're having. Some examples are happy, sad, angry, and afraid.

Thoughts

When you notice that a trigger has set off body sensations or emotions, ask yourself, *What am I thinking right now?* Thoughts are powerful. They can make feelings better or worse, and they can influence what you do (your behaviors).

Behaviors

What you do and what you say — any actions you take — are responses to triggers. These can include behaviors you feel control over, such as apologizing, or behaviors you don't feel control over, like crying.

Once you know what's happening on the Feelings Pathway, you can do something about it. Let's take a closer look on the next page.

WORKING TOGETHER

Here's how the Feelings Pathway and coping tools work together. The Feelings Pathway helps you become more aware of how a stress trigger affects you. Once you're aware, you can use coping tools to transform that stress trigger from overwhelming to under control.

Let's pretend you have a class presentation tomorrow. Whenever you think about it, your stomach does somersaults. Using the Feelings Pathway helps you notice that body sensation — and then you can explore what thoughts, emotions, and behaviors are connected to it.

TRIGGER: Stress because of class presentation

- **BEHAVIOR:** Biting nails, saying you won't go to school
- **BODY SENSATION:** Stomach doing somersaults
- **EMOTION:** Worry, fear
- **THOUGHT:** *I might screw up*

Now that you know these answers, test what coping tools help you feel better. Finding the right ones can transform the stress trigger from feeling overwhelming to feeling under control. For example, to change your thoughts, you might use an In Your Head coping tool ("everyone gets nervous," see pages 32 and 59). Or to calm your stomach, you might try an In Your Body coping tool (three deep breaths, see page 76).

It's OK and normal to feel nervous about a class presentation, but you don't want the stress to have all the power. Coping tools are your magic wands that give you control over how stress affects how you think, feel, and act.

Now that you've been introduced to triggers, coping, and the Feelings Pathway, let's explore nine of the most common emotions.

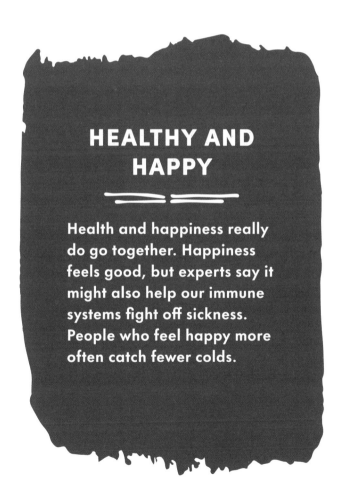

HEALTHY AND HAPPY

Health and happiness really do go together. Happiness feels good, but experts say it might also help our immune systems fight off sickness. People who feel happy more often catch fewer colds.

CHAPTER 1
HAPPINESS

FEELING HAPPY FEELS GOOD.

Have you ever noticed just how wonderful you feel doing your favorite activity or being with your favorite people? Everyone wants to be happy, so you might wonder why you're not always happy. And when you're feeling sad, you might think something is wrong. You might feel pressure from family and friends (or anyone!) to just cheer up, no matter what. Maybe you think you're just not a happy type of person. But here's a secret: Happy is not a type of person.

Happiness is temporary. It comes and goes like the sunshine, which can be bright and then fade behind clouds. It's OK and *normal* if you're not happy all the time. But noticing and really appreciating the happy moments can help you remember that the warmth of the sunshine still exists even when it's behind the clouds.

Taking a minute to notice and appreciate these good moments — being excited about a big trip, enjoying a great book, having a random dance party with your family — can help you better handle stress and difficult times when they come. Scientists say people who regularly notice pleasant moments feel happiness more often and build inner strength, or resilience.

The exercises throughout this chapter will help you plant happiness seeds so that you can grow a garden of resilience around you. It's not realistic to try to be happy all the time, but you can make sure your happiness plants have strong roots. Knowing and caring for your own happiness helps you feel confident and hopeful even on those days when the clouds hide the sunshine.

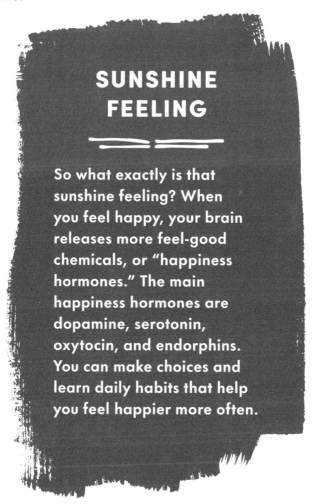

SUNSHINE FEELING

So what exactly is that sunshine feeling? When you feel happy, your brain releases more feel-good chemicals, or "happiness hormones." The main happiness hormones are dopamine, serotonin, oxytocin, and endorphins. You can make choices and learn daily habits that help you feel happier more often.

MAKE A LIST OF SOME OF YOUR BIG AND SMALL HAPPY MOMENTS.

BIG

HAPPY MOMENTS

....

....

....

....

....

....

....

....

Knowing what makes you light up can help on hard days: You can look back at this list and remember that there are good moments, not just difficult ones, or find ideas to add a dose of sunshine to your cloudy day.

HAPPY MOMENTS

DRAW A PICTURE OF WHAT YOU LOOK LIKE WHEN YOU'RE HAPPY.

Drawing a feeling can help you be *in* that feeling as you re-create the moment that you experienced it. What are you doing, where are you, and is anyone with you? Remember, there's no right way to make this drawing; draw whatever feels right to you!

LIST WHO MAKES YOU FEEL GOOD.

Connection
Coping Tool

Physical affection, like hugs and feeling closer to friends and family, is an important source of happiness for everyone. Record the people below who make you smile. When you need a dose of happiness, go to them!

INCLUDE YOUR PETS!

1. ....

2. ....

3. ....

4. ....

5. ....

6. ....

7. ....

8. ....

9. ....

10. ....

PRACTICE THE POWER OF POSITIVE THINKING.

Scientists have discovered that being optimistic — having positive and hopeful thoughts about the future — helps us live healthier. But thoughts that are *just* optimistic won't do: positive thoughts must also be possible and realistic to help you actually feel better.

At right, circle the positive statements that are possible and realistic. Hint: Some might seem realistic, but think about whether you would believe them when you're feeling nervous or upset.

NOW TRY THIS!

What positive thoughts do you believe about yourself that would give you a boost on a bad day? A positive statement about yourself that you repeat over and over is called a mantra, like: "I am important." "I am loved." Craft your own mantras below:

START WITH AN "I" STATEMENT

....

....

....

....

....

FOR WHEN YOU'RE NERVOUS ABOUT A HARD TEST

"Of course I'm going to ace this test!"

"I have studied and am ready to do my best on this test."

FOR WHEN SOMETHING SEEMS HARD

"I have done hard things before, and I can handle this."

"Everything will be fine no matter what."

FOR WHEN YOU MAKE A MISTAKE

"Mistakes help me learn, and everyone makes mistakes."

"I will never make another mistake."

FOR PREPARING FOR A BIG GAME

"I'm the best player on the team."

"I practice and work hard to be a good team player."

FOR WHEN YOU HAVE A FIGHT WITH A FRIEND

"I'll never upset my friend again."

"I will keep doing my best to be a good friend."

THINK ABOUT HOW YOU HELP.

Write about a time when you helped friends, family, or other people around you.

....

....

....

....

....

....

....

....

....

It turns out that, according to brain science, we feel good when we're kind and helpful to others. In fact, when you act for the sake of others instead of for yourself, your brain wants you to do it again and again to keep getting that happy feeling.

DOGGY LANGUAGE

Want to know how your dog really feels? Watch their tail. We usually interpret a wagging tail as the sign of a happy dog, but scientists have discovered that a lot depends on which direction the tail is moving. If the tail wags more to the right, the dog is feeling friendly and happy. But if it wags to the left, the dog might be more stressed and anxious. When a dog shakes their whole butt with their tail? Then they are very happy!

PICTURE YOURSELF OUTSIDE.

Draw your favorite outdoor place, and fill in what you see, hear, and smell when you're there.

I see ....

I hear ....

I smell ....

Focusing on the smells, sounds, and sights of outdoor spaces is sometimes called taking a nature bath! Nature baths can lower stress hormones and help you feel better overall.

CHAPTER 2
SADNESS

EVERYONE FEELS SAD SOMETIMES.

Having sad moments is a part of life. You could feel sad if a friend leaves you out or your parents are fighting, or when you say goodbye to your favorite teacher.

Most people think of sadness as crying, feeling down, or having low energy. But sadness can also come out as feeling irritable. *Irritable* means getting angry or annoyed at small things, like the weird way your sibling looks at you or how your friend chews their food. If you notice being annoyed more often than usual, check in with yourself. Is there something you might be feeling sad about?

Sadness isn't fun or enjoyable, so it makes sense that people try to avoid feeling sad. But avoiding bad feelings actually causes more bad feelings—the frustration and effort of keeping that sadness stuffed deep down might come out as an angry eruption. Instead of distracting yourself, try to let yourself feel sad when sadness comes. In the end, it helps your brain learn that sadness won't hurt you: You can feel sad and then feel better again. The activities in this chapter will give you more ideas for how to understand and cope with your sadness so you take care of it in healthy ways.

CAN YOU BE TOO SAD?

Everyone feels sad from time to time, but if you feel sad or irritable most of the time over a couple of weeks, let an adult know. If you feel this way and you have no idea why, talking to an adult can also help keep it from getting worse.

MAKE A LIST OF SOME OF YOUR BIG AND SMALL SAD MOMENTS.

BIG
SAD MOMENTS

....

....

....

....

....

....

....

....

....

Just as you did for happy moments, think of times you've felt sad in your life. You might even discover that some small sad moments are connected to the big ones. After making your lists, review them to help you know your sadness triggers.

SAD MOMENTS

....

....

....

....

....

....

....

....

....

RETHINK YOUR SAD THOUGHTS.

Negative thoughts can make sadness feel worse or make you feel stuck in your sadness. But you can talk back to negative thoughts using balanced thinking. Write down your negative thought. Then rewrite it to make it more encouraging and realistic. Both thoughts recognize the trigger, but the balanced thought helps you cope with it. To get started, check out the example below.

SAD THOUGHT
"I'm never going to see my best friend again after she moves away."

→

BALANCED THOUGHT
"It won't be the same, but we will come up with ways to stay close. We can FaceTime after school, and I can talk to my parents about how to see them on the weekend."

SAD THOUGHT
"I totally messed up that final play and let down my whole team."

→

BALANCED THOUGHT
"I feel so bad that I blew that play! But I know what to do next time. Even the greatest athletes make mistakes."

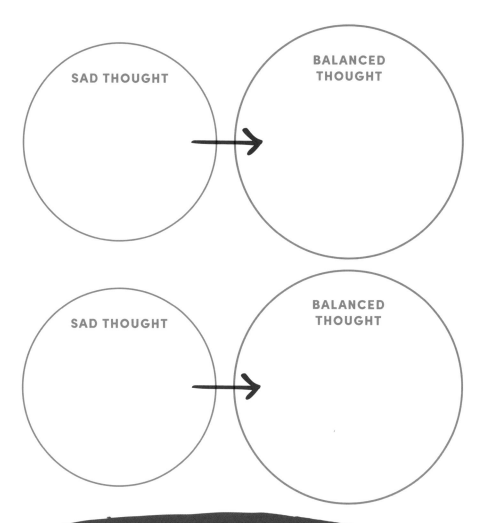

SAD THOUGHT → BALANCED THOUGHT

SAD THOUGHT → BALANCED THOUGHT

THE GOOD SIDE OF SADNESS

Happiness may feel pleasant, but sadness can help us too. Sadness may let you know what's important to you in life. For example, if a person you love gets ill, it's sad, but it also reminds you of how important that relationship is to you.

ACCEPT THE RAIN.

Sadness is often an uncomfortable emotion for people. When you feel sad, close your eyes and imagine your sadness is like a rainstorm that has a beginning and an end. Listen to the rain start to come down harder, and feel the sadness get stronger. Then listen to the rain become lighter and fade away until it's gone, and feel the sadness lighten too. Write about how you felt while your eyes were closed.

THIS CAN WORK FOR ANY UNCOMFORTABLE EMOTION, LIKE ANGER OR JEALOUSY.

....

....

....

....

....

....

....

....

....

SADNESS LOOKS LIKE...

Draw your sadness as if it were a person or a creature (and include as many details as possible!). Give them a name and add yourself to the picture, looking like friends in a comfy and cozy spot. Your finished scene is a reminder to get comfortable with your sadness.

DRAW A MASK THAT YOU WEAR WHEN YOU FEEL SAD.

Sadness can wear disguises, like anger or frustration. Does your mask have those emotions or other ways of appearing? Or do you pretend like everything is OK and try to smile your way through the sadness in front of other people?

The next time you realize you're wearing this mask, see if you can say to yourself, *I'm actually really sad even though I'm acting [angry/quiet/OK]*. Then let someone know you're actually not OK. See how it feels to take off the mask and be honest about your sadness.

WHEN SADNESS IS HELPFUL

Sadness can motivate us more than happiness. When you feel happy, you are content and comfortable and want to stay that way. Feeling sad lets you know there's something you want to do differently, and it can push you to make it happen.

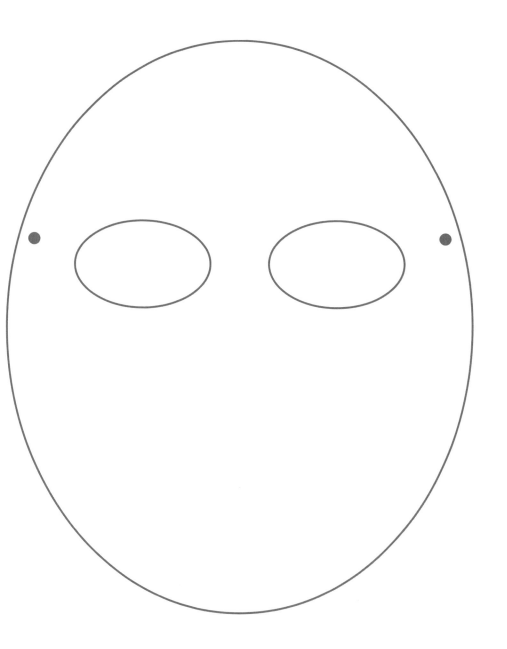

WRITE A LETTER TO SOMEONE YOU TRUST.

Expression and Connection Coping Tool

Think of a time you felt really sad recently (maybe it's even right now). Pick someone you trust in your life — another kid or an adult — and write a letter to them about your sadness. Describe what happened, why it makes you sad, and how your sadness feels.

(You never have to actually show this letter to anyone, but it's good practice to express your emotions.)

Dear .... ,

....

....

....

....

....

....

....

....

....

....

....

....

....

....

....

....

....

....

....

From your friend,

....

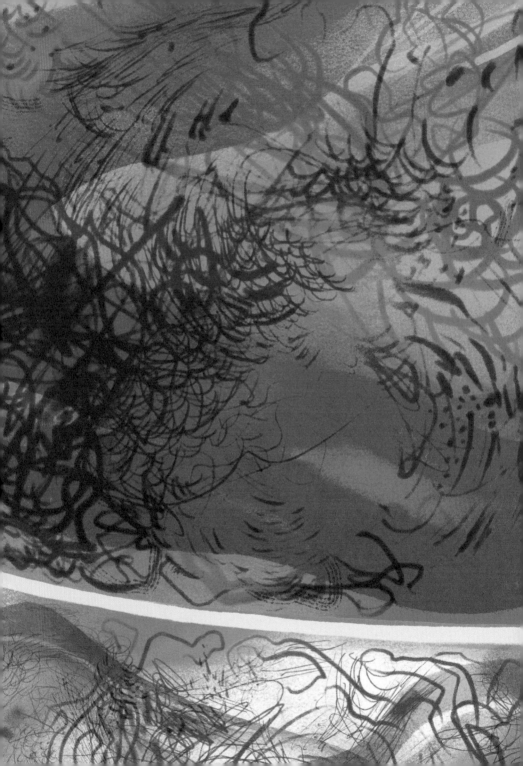

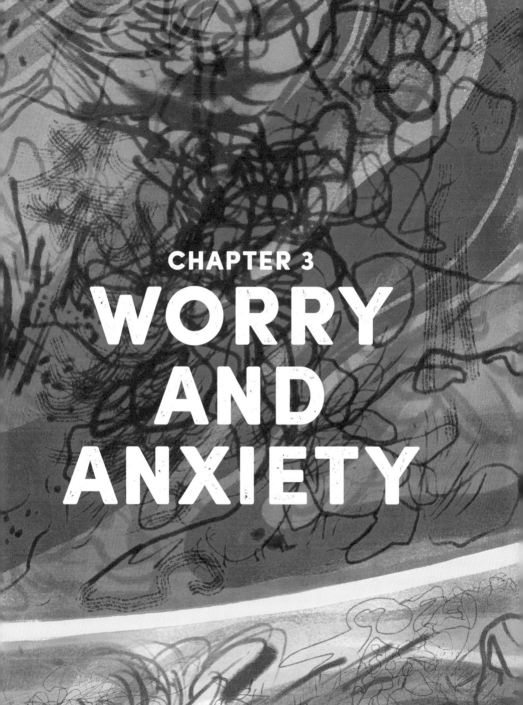

CHAPTER 3

WORRY AND ANXIETY

THERE'S A LOT TO WORRY ABOUT THESE DAYS...

Identifying and understanding your worries can help you manage them so they don't take over your life.

What exactly is a worry? Worries are thoughts that focus on what might happen in the future and usually cause stress. They come in small or big packages — such as *What if I get questions wrong on my homework?* or *What if my best friend doesn't want to be friends anymore?*

Did you notice what's the same about both of those thoughts? They start with *what if* and end with stuff you *don't* want to happen. That's what makes them worries.

Often, when you're worried about something specific, you can either let it go or do something to help the worry go away, like asking your parent to look over your homework before turning it in. Worries usually come and go, and there are tools you can use to help your worries not get too stuck. Everyone has worries, but they don't have to take over your brain!

WHEN WORRY BECOMES ANXIETY

~~~

When worries start piling up in your head and you can't control them, you might be dealing with anxiety. If you try these coping strategies and still feel anxious, let an adult know you might need more help.

MAKE A LIST OF YOUR
BIG AND SMALL WORRIES.

We never know what's going to happen in the future, so it's natural to worry. Making this list can help you identify your worry triggers.

....

....

....

....

....

....

....

NOW TRY THIS.

Look at each worry and ask yourself: "Do I think about this even when I don't want to?" If you can't focus because you're worried, the worry is controlling you. Circle the worries that you can't stop from spinning around in your brain. Try using the **FEELINGS PATHWAY** for one so it doesn't take over your mind and turn into anxiety, or talk to an adult you trust about how you feel.

WORRIES

....

....

....

....

....

....

....

SCHEDULE WORRY TIME.

Set a timer for 15 minutes, and let your worries race around your brain. When the timer goes off, do your best to stop worrying and turn your thoughts to other things. Draw what your brain looks like with all the worries racing around and then what it looks like when you stop the timer.

BEFORE   **AFTER**

If a worry comes back, remind yourself that you had your worry time today and you can think about it again during your worry time tomorrow. This helps your mind practice letting go of worries — even the ones that are hard to control.

FLIP THE WORRY SCRIPT.

In Your Head
Coping Tool

Challenge yourself to rework the "what if" worries to end in positives. Write your "what if" worry on the left and change it to a positive one on the right.

"WHAT IF" WORRIES

"WHAT IF" AWESOMENESS

What if I freeze in front of my class tomorrow during my presentation?

What if I crush my class presentation tomorrow?

BREATHE YOUR WORRIES AWAY.

On the tree below, write down a worry on each leaf. Next, close your eyes and take five deep breaths. When you breathe out, imagine one worry leaf floating away until there are no more leaves on the tree.

CIRCLE WHERE IN YOUR BODY YOU FEEL WORRY OR ANXIETY.

In Your Body Coping Tool

Next to the spots, describe the sensation—for example, "My hands are sweaty." The next time you feel these sensations, check in with yourself to see if you're feeling nervous, then use the breathing strategy on the previous page to help the body release the anxious feelings.

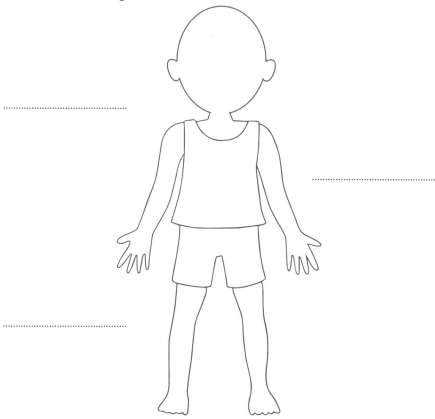

GET GROUNDED.

No, it's not what happens when you break your parents' rules! Grounding means using your senses to be fully aware of the moment. This helps your mind focus on the present and not worry about the future.

You can tune in to your five senses anywhere if you need a few seconds to get calm and focused. Paying attention to your senses can switch your mind away from worries.

If you're in class, for example, you could notice the following:

> **FEEL** the pencil in your hand.
> **HEAR** the clock ticking.
> **SEE** the kid next to you.
> **SMELL** the laundry scent on your T-shirt.
> **TASTE** water from your water bottle.

Don't worry about which sense to activate first—just notice whatever gets your attention, and go in any order you want!

Now let's practice! To the right, record what you feel, hear, see, smell, and taste.

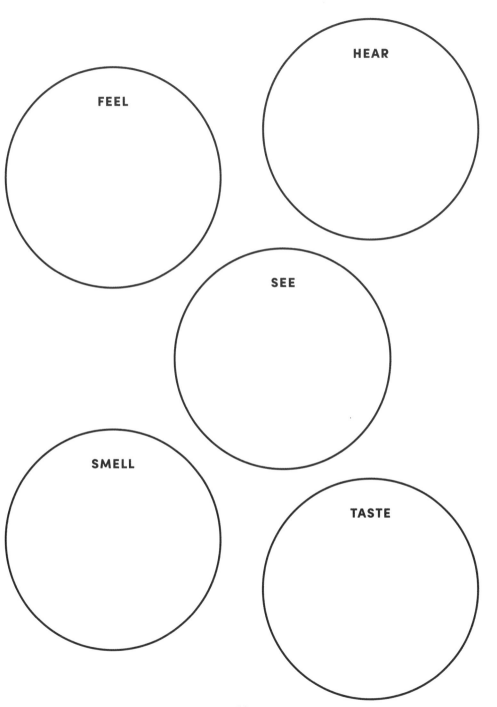

FEEL

HEAR

SEE

SMELL

TASTE

THE UPSIDE OF WORRY: SOLVING PROBLEMS.

In Your Head
Coping Tool

Fill in the columns below with moments when a worry motivated you to solve a challenge.

MY WORRY

MY SOLUTION

Even though feeling worried can be unpleasant, it can let you know there's a problem you need to solve. The next time you feel worried, think about this list and get ideas for how to solve a problem. You'll know that you can come up with a solution for a new worry because you've done it before.

CHAPTER 4
ANGER

YOU CAN CONTROL YOUR ANGER.

Have you ever slammed a door, thrown something, or punched or kicked when you're angry? A small almond-shaped part of the brain called the **amygdala** is where anger flares up, sending a rush of energy to the body to tell it to fight. Fighting is the body's natural response to anger—which is why anger and being aggressive often happen together: Anger is the emotion and aggression is the behavior.

The brain is built to get angry. And while slamming, throwing, screaming, and yelling are behaviors linked to anger, it prompts helpful behaviors too. For example, a main trigger for anger is feeling like something isn't fair. (If you have a sibling, you probably know this feeling well!) When a situation feels unfair—especially in a community—anger can help people take action to make a change, such as starting a dialogue or organizing a peaceful demonstration.

The risky part of anger is when it makes people feel out of control, which happens to just about everyone at one time or another. It feels pretty terrible.

Because of brain and personality differences, some people feel anger more strongly and act out more when they're mad. When people are angry, they may hurt others with their bodies (physical aggression) or their words (yelling hurtful comments). As with sadness, sometimes people try to stuff down their anger, but that's not healthy either. It's important to learn how to cope with anger so you express it *safely*—without hurting yourself or others.

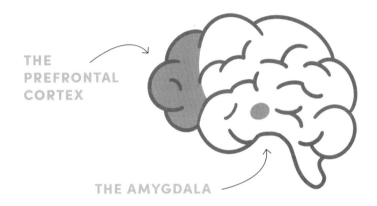

THE PREFRONTAL CORTEX

THE AMYGDALA

YOUR GROWING BRAIN

Most kids have angrier outbursts than adults because of how the brain grows. As you get older, your brain will get better at feeling anger without immediately acting on it thanks to your growing **prefrontal cortex** (the part of your brain right behind your forehead). That's where thinking and making good choices happen. The prefrontal cortex tells the angry amygdala: "Chill out! Stop before you act!" Your prefrontal cortex's chill-out powers are still growing, and using coping tools can help your prefrontal cortex get stronger.

THINK OF TIMES YOU'VE FELT FRUSTRATED...

...like when you can't find the remote or you keep making small mistakes on your history homework even though you know you understand it.

Feeling frustrated often comes before the stronger feeling of anger. In fact, you can think of frustration like a small firecracker that could set off a big angry firework. **BOOM!** If you learn to notice frustration, you can work on settling it down before it becomes anger.

List some of your frustration firecrackers on the next page, plus what happens or could happen if that firecracker explodes an anger firework. Use your imagination for how big you could make the firework explode if you got really, really angry! Thinking about how out of control your anger can get is a helpful reminder to contain it before you hurt someone (including yourself).

FRUSTRATION
FIRECRACKERS

ANGRY
FIREWORKS

I couldn't find my favorite shirt that I really wanted to wear.

I threw every piece of clothing from my closet in the trash. (Then you wouldn't have any clothes!)

WHICH OF THESE COMMON TRIGGERS ANGER YOU?

Use a bright-red marker to circle the ones that turn up your anger dial to the highest volume! Add your own anger triggers to the empty bubbles.

FEELING LIKE SOMETHING IS UNFAIR

LOSING

NOT BEING LISTENED TO

SOMEONE HURTING PEOPLE YOU CARE ABOUT

SOMEONE HURTING YOU

NOT GETTING WHAT YOU WANT

BEING TEASED

FEELING LIKE PEOPLE DON'T UNDERSTAND YOU

GETTING LEFT OUT

VIDEO GAME OR SCREEN TIME ENDING

NAME WHAT'S FLOWING LIKE LAVA FROM YOUR ANGER VOLCANO.

Anger is often the top layer of other emotions that people don't like feeling, such as sadness, fear, or worry. When you ignore those other emotions, the anger keeps bubbling inside to eventually explode — like lava out of a volcano.

Think about times you have felt angry and ask yourself what other emotions may have been bubbling below the surface of your anger. (Jealousy? Embarrassment? Sadness? Fear?) Write them in the red lava on the volcano.

BE SILLY!

Laughter really is the best medicine — for anger. Finding something funny in the middle of feeling angry can actually make that anger fire go right out, like blowing out a candle. Do something silly the next time your sibling or friend starts to get heated, and see what happens.

PRACTICE BALLOON BREATHING.

Taking deep breaths, or balloon breathing, is a great way to prevent frustration from turning into anger. To do this exercise, picture a balloon inside your belly: When you breathe in, the balloon fills up; when you breathe out, it deflates. Make your breaths long by counting slowly to three when you breathe in, and slowly to four for when you breathe out. As you practice, you can count even higher for longer inhales and exhales. You might not notice a difference right away, but keep going! The more often you practice balloon breathing, the better it works.

Think of a time of day that your body feels the most tired, or when you feel the grumpiest, or when your mind has a lot of worries (perhaps that's in the morning, right when school starts, or after the school day ends). Start a habit of taking three balloon breaths at the same time each day. Before you know it, you'll feel calmer and more focused in those tough times!

I plan to practice balloon breathing when:

....

....

....

....

ARE YOU UNSURE WHAT A DEEP BREATH FEELS LIKE?

Lie down and put an object (like a stuffed animal) on your stomach, and make sure it moves up and down when you inhale and exhale, so you know the breath is moving from your stomach and not from your chest. After you learn how deep breathing feels, you can do it anywhere — sitting, standing, or lying down — for any tough emotion, not just anger. The best part is that breathing is quiet, so nobody needs to know if you don't want them to! It's easy to do in class or at a soccer game, or anytime you start to feel stress or a strong emotion building. In the balloons below, write down when balloon breathing could help you. Before a test? When your sibling frustrates you? To help you fall asleep?

FIND YOUR YOUR ANGER STYLE.

SITUATION: A kid in your class often picks on other kids, including you. They make mean jokes and make people feel bad. One day, they make fun of you when you're tagged out in a game at recess. Of course this makes you angry!

Circle the response below that most closely matches what you would do in this situation. Then learn about your anger style and other anger styles on the next page.

A. Tell some friends a rumor about the kid that isn't true but that you know will be hurtful.

B. Hold in your anger even though you feel tears, walk away, and act like it doesn't bother you.

C. Start shoving and calling the kid names.

D. Speak up without losing control or being mean: "Hey, everyone gets out in this game. You don't need to be so mean about it. Nobody likes it when you say that stuff."

IF YOU PICKED A: You might have a **passive-aggressive** anger style. This means you express anger indirectly, such as ignoring the person or saying mean things about them to others.

IF YOU PICKED B: You might have a **passive** anger style. This means you keep the anger inside and don't react, so the other person doesn't know you're angry.

IF YOU PICKED C: You might have an **aggressive** anger style. This means you attack the person physically, verbally make threats, or destroy objects.

IF YOU PICKED D: You might have an **assertive** anger style. This means you speak up for yourself or others by being clear and firm but without attacking the other person.

Disagreement or conflict with another person is a common trigger for anger. It's normal to have some conflict with people in your life. But how you manage your anger and communicate during disagreements can affect whether conflict is healthy and leads to a solution or unhealthy and leads to more problems.

WHICH ONE DO YOU THINK IS THE HEALTHIEST FOR YOU?

If you guessed Assertive, you are correct! You calmly express yourself and nobody gets hurt.

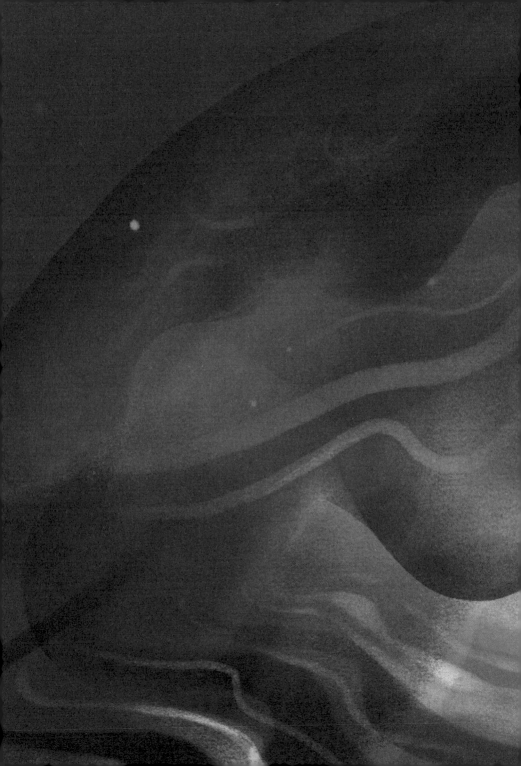

CHAPTER 5
GRIEF

GRIEF IS ABOUT LOSS.

Have you ever had a big change in your life? Maybe your family moved, you switched schools, or a close friend no longer lives next door. Even though most people think of grief as what you feel when someone dies, grief comes up for all kinds of loss. During the COVID-19 pandemic, a lot of kids and teens felt grief over not being able to see their friends in person or over missing a special school event like graduation. Other big life changes — parents' separating or divorcing, a sibling becoming seriously ill — can also trigger grief. Grief can happen when you miss your life before a big change happened.

It's common to think grief is a type of sadness, but grief includes lots of emotions swirled together. It feels like really deep sadness, but it also involves moments of strong anger. Grief makes bodies feel heavy and tired. It can also come and go in surprising ways. You might feel normal, and then suddenly the grief washes over you like a big wave.

How do you know if you're grieving? Grief sends extra cortisol (a stress hormone) through the body to affect many parts of how it works. Many grieving people have trouble eating and sleeping, and they feel more tired than usual. You may notice missing how life used to be (like when your whole family lived together or you got to see your best friend every day). These thoughts may pop up when you're supposed to be concentrating on other things, like what your teacher is saying in class. But it's important to know that even though these are common ways to feel grief, there is no one way to grieve. Some people may feel more sadness, others more anger. Some people may get easily distracted by having fun, others may not be able to have fun. This is why it's important to get to know *your* grief.

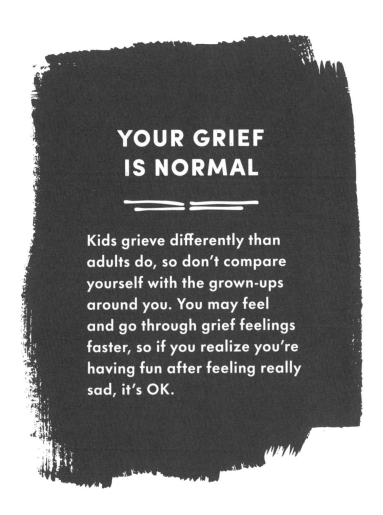

YOUR GRIEF IS NORMAL

Kids grieve differently than adults do, so don't compare yourself with the grown-ups around you. You may feel and go through grief feelings faster, so if you realize you're having fun after feeling really sad, it's OK.

THINK ABOUT YOUR EXPERIENCE OF GRIEF AND LOSS.

Reflect on big changes in your life that may have been hard to get used to, or pets or people you love who have died. List some of these losses here.

LOSSES OR DIFFICULT CHANGES I'VE EXPERIENCED

....

....

....

....

....

....

....

....

....

....

Go deeper and journal about one of your losses here. Describe what happened, how it made you feel, and how you feel about it now.

....

....

....

....

....

....

....

....

....

....

....

....

....

....

MAKE A LIST OF PEOPLE WHO MAKE YOU FEEL BETTER.

Connection
Coping Tool

Grieving can feel really lonely, as if nobody else can understand. This list is here when you need it and reminds you that you're not alone: These people care about you even if you feel lonely in grief.

1. ....

2. ....

3. ....

4. ....

5. ....

6. ....

7. ....

8. ....

9. ....

10. ....

Your list might change as you get older, so use a pencil and update it as needed.

If you find people who have gone through a similar loss — like the death of a family member — this can be especially helpful in feeling less alone. Put a star next to the name of anyone who can really get what you're going through because they've lived through something similar.

NOT YOUR FAULT

Sometimes you might blame yourself for a sad event, like a divorce or death, even though you had nothing to do with it. Emotions can trick the mind into believing things that aren't true. If you're feeling this way, the best thing you can do is share with a trusted adult.

WHAT WOULD YOU PUT IN A MEMORY BOX?

Rituals like making memory boxes — decorated containers where you can put objects that honor your loss — can help ease painful moments in grief. Draw or write about a few items that you would put in your memory box to honor your memories about what you lost, such as a pet's collar, a card from a grandparent, or photos of your old house. Make notes about why these objects are special.

THESE ITEMS REMIND ME OF: ....

....

HOW TO MAKE A MEMORY BOX

1. Pick a box that feels right to you. It could be a shoebox or a gift box that's just the right size and shape.

2. Decide whether you want to decorate the outside of the box. You could paint it with colors or images that remind you of who or what you want to remember, make a collage by cutting out and gluing on pictures from magazines, or even decorate it with your own photos.

3. Think about objects that remind you of your memories. The objects could have belonged to the person or pet you're grieving, or they could be your own belongings that bring you comfort when you think of the loss, such as a card with a poem from the funeral service or a gift from your loved one.

4. Keep this memory box private, to open when you have a quiet moment, or share it with others as a way to talk about your memories and feelings. Or do both — it's your choice.

WORK OUT YOUR GRIEF

Exercise can help a lot with grief because it releases the stress chemical cortisol, which grief increases in our bodies.

WRITE A LETTER TO WHOMEVER OR WHATEVER YOU'RE MISSING.

Expression and Connection Coping Tool

Finding meaning is a big part of coping with grief. Think about how that person, animal, or experience made your life better even though the loved one is gone or the experience is over.

Dear ....,

....

....

....

....

....

....

....

....

....

....

....

....

....

....

....

....

....

....

....

....

....

....

From your friend,

....

CREATE YOUR GRIEF MANDALA.

Grief is an emotion *full* of other emotions. Most grief-related emotions, such as loneliness, confusion, and guilt, feel difficult. But others, such as gratitude and love, can feel positive too — and that's OK (some people feel guilty if they feel positive emotions when grieving).

A mandala may look like a simple circle, but it is also a powerful symbol of finding meaning in life, which is something grief often helps people uncover. Think about which emotions on the list at right are true for your grief. (You can ignore the ones that don't apply to you.) Then pick a color for each emotion that is part of your grief and fill in the circle with every color. The more of one color the circle has, the stronger that feeling is as part of your grief. You can even blend colors together.

EXAMPLE:

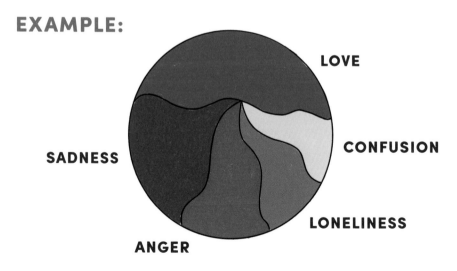

LOVE

CONFUSION

SADNESS

LONELINESS

ANGER

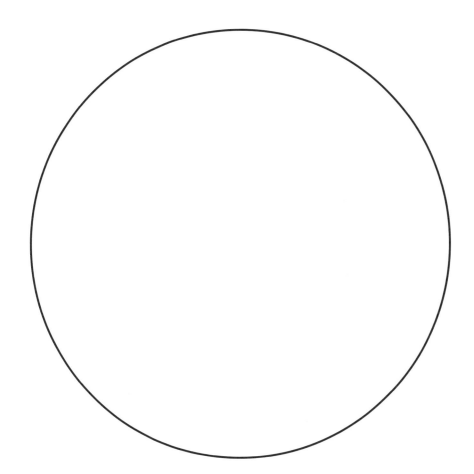

MY COLOR FOR...

- ○ Love
- ○ Sadness
- ○ Anger
- ○ Confusion
- ○ Frustration
- ○ Gratitude
- ○ Loneliness

- ○ Anxiety
- ○ Guilt
- ○ Fear
- ○ Worry
- ○ ....
- ○ ....
- ○ ....

COLOR IT IN!

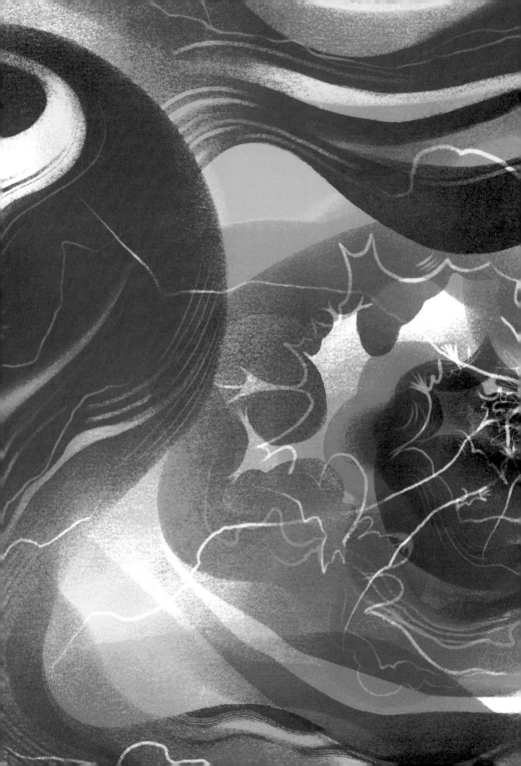

CHAPTER 6
EMBARRASSMENT

EVERYONE GETS EMBARRASSED.

You spill a drink down your shirt at lunch, get an answer wrong in front of the class, or make a joke that nobody laughs at—your face gets red, you start to sweat, and boy, do you feel *embarrassed*.

Embarrassment is called a "self-conscious" emotion because it's caused by your thoughts about how other people see you.

Even though it's not so fun to feel, embarrassment happens for a reason: It helps us learn how to belong to a group. Embarrassing moments are usually when you do something against what's expected—from tripping and falling in front of a roomful of people to forgetting your lines on stage in the school play.

In the moment, embarrassment is awful. But that feeling helps you know what to do next time you're in a similar social situation. For example, if you call someone you've met before by the wrong name, next time you will pay closer attention when someone introduces themselves.

Being too hard on yourself when you're feeling embarrassed can lead to other tough emotions like guilt and shame (which you'll read more about in the next chapter). Instead, try to remember that when you feel embarrassed, you're usually much more aware of it than anyone else. Even better: By understanding embarrassment and how to cope with it, you can even turn an embarrassing moment into a way to bond with others!

The most important thing to remember about embarrassment? Every single person goes through it.

LAUGH IT OFF

Scientists have found out that if you can laugh off an embarrassing moment, the people around you see you as likable and someone to trust. So the next time you trip in front of a bunch of people, laugh about it, say "I meant to do that," and see what happens!

LIST YOUR MOST CRINGEWORTHY EMBARRASSING MOMENTS.

Ugh. They can be so mortifying to even think about, let alone write down. But by looking at this list of truly uncomfortable moments all together, you might see patterns — like two moments having the same trigger. And remember: This book is for your eyes only!

1. ....
....

2. ....
....

3. ....
....

4. ....
....

5. ....
....

COLOR WHERE IN YOUR BODY YOU FEEL EMBARRASSED.

Next to the spots, describe the sensation—for example, "my cheeks get red." You can use deep breathing to help your body and mind settle down when embarrassed!

GET A HANDLE ON YOUR EMBARRASSMENT DIAL.

In Your Head
Coping Tool

Imagine this embarrassing moment: It's your turn to present your book report in front of the class. You start talking and completely forget what you practiced! You make up some stuff to say, but you stumble over your words and feel like everyone is judging you. You sit back down feeling totally embarrassed. What do you do? Draw an arrow pointing to your reaction on the embarrassment meter below.

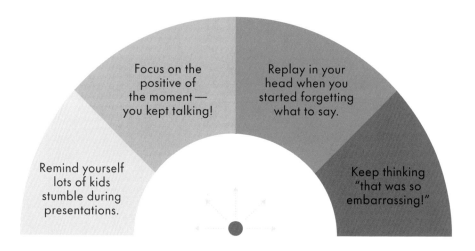

In an embarrassing moment, you can react and either make the feeling worse (turning the embarrassment dial up) or make it go away sooner (turning the embarrassment dial down).

FIND OUT WHAT MATTERS MOST TO YOU.

Being embarrassed can help you know what you care about most. Fill in the chart below with embarrassing moments, and include what you cared about in that moment and what you could do next time to avoid embarrassment.

EMBARRASSING MOMENT	WHAT I CARED ABOUT	WHAT I CAN DO NEXT TIME
Shooting the basketball in the wrong hoop.	Being a good teammate.	Pay closer attention to which hoop is ours.

BE AN EMBARRASSMENT DETECTIVE.

Connection
Coping Tool

One way to challenge embarrassment is to tell yourself that it happens to everyone. Interview others about their most embarrassing stories (and share your own with them!). Write down your best discoveries here. And don't forget to laugh with each other!

EMBARRASSMENT DISCOVERY #1

....

....

....

....

....

> **Think back to an embarrassing moment. How long did the feeling last? Even though embarrassment feels intense, it usually doesn't last long. So the next time you're embarrassed, it will help if you can remind yourself, "This will be over soon!"**

EMBARRASSMENT DISCOVERY #2

....

....

....

....

....

....

EMBARRASSMENT DISCOVERY #3

....

....

....

....

....

....

CHAPTER 7
GUILT

HAVE YOU EVER FELT GUILTY?

Hint: humans are built to feel guilt, so the answer is probably yes. For example, you may feel guilty if you broke your sibling's toy in a moment of anger. Guilt can also be triggered by a secret that nobody knows about but you — like maybe you cheated on a test and didn't get caught, but you feel guilty because you know cheating is wrong.

People often think of guilt as a bad emotion. But if you pay attention to it, it can help you. Guilt usually tells you that you did something that you wish you hadn't done, and if you admit this, you can take steps to correct the mistake, like apologizing for hurting someone's feelings or confessing to a teacher that you lied about losing your homework.

Plus, feeling guilty usually shows that you have an important skill called empathy. Empathy means you understand how another person would feel, even if it's different from how you feel — so if you feel guilty, you care about how the other person feels. Guilt does not have to be overwhelming; it's pretty easy to take action to move through guilt and feel better.

NO SHAME

Shame is a stronger emotion and longer-lasting than embarrassment or guilt because it's tied to who you think you are rather than something you did. The challenge with overcoming shame is that people don't often want to talk about it. By not expressing shameful thoughts and feelings, they can get stuck in your head and make you feel terrible about yourself.

WHAT DO YOU FEEL GUILTY ABOUT?

Expression
Coping Tool

Write down what makes you feel guilty. Because this is your private space, you can be honest. These are your guilt triggers. You can use the activities in the rest of the chapter to figure out how to cope with the guilt.

1. ....

....

2. ....

....

3. ....

....

4. ....

....

5. ....

....

NOW WRITE A CONFESSION.

Expression
Coping Tool

Pick one guilt trigger from the previous page and fill this page
with all the details about it: what happened, who was involved,
what you said or did, how you felt, and why you feel guilty about
it. After you write about the experience, notice how you feel.
People often feel relief when they admit a guilty secret.

CHANGE GUILTY THOUGHTS INTO KINDER THOUGHTS.

In Your Head
Coping Tool

A behavior is not who you are as a person. You can do things that make you feel guilty, and still have great qualities like being a kind friend or a helpful sibling. Transform your guilt below. Self-compassion is the best medicine.

GUILT TRIGGER	GUILTY THOUGHT	KINDER THOUGHT
Yelled at my friend.	*"I'm such a bad friend!"*	*"I lost my temper, but I'm usually a good friend. We all make mistakes."*

GUILT TRIGGER	GUILTY THOUGHT	KINDER THOUGHT

TELL A GUILT STORY.

Use your creativity and imagination to weave a story about a main character who does something they feel super guilty about. Include what happened before the guilty moment and during the guilty incident and what the character did afterward to cope with it. Use your imagination to come up with fun characters and make the guilty incident as big as possible! Feel free to add your own illustrations.

GOOD GUILT

Guilt has helped humans stay alive as a species because it triggers people to treat each other better.

CHAPTER 8
PRIDE

FEELING PROUD IS GOOD FOR YOU!

Pride can come from accomplishing a goal, being praised and told you've done well, or being part of a group — like a team that has worked hard all season. Being proud of yourself is an important part of feeling good about who you are and your skills (self-esteem). Everyone has their own skills and strengths that should be celebrated!

Scientists have discovered that pride helps people not only reach their goals but also act kinder. For example, if you write a poem for your friend on their birthday and your friend loves it, this makes your friend happy and like you more *and* you feel proud that they liked it. Everyone feels great!

But sometimes being proud of yourself can seem rude or like you think you're better than others. Scientists have figured out that there are two ways of having pride: One is positive and healthy for your self-esteem ("authentic pride"), and the other is negative and makes people not like you ("arrogant pride"). Authentic pride can be part of confidence and achieving goals. These exercises will help you develop a positive outlook about yourself and your accomplishments.

BEING PROUD
WITHOUT BRAGGING

· · · · · · · · · · · · · ·

Wondering how to express feeling proud
without coming off the wrong way?
Here's how to avoid sounding as if you're
exaggerating the truth:

Imagine you won a race.

1. Talk about your effort: "I practiced
   every day" instead of "It was so easy."

2. Stay focused on yourself instead of
   others: "I got first place!" instead
   of "I was faster than everybody else."

3. Mention anyone who helped you: "My
   parents gave me good advice about
   how to get ready for the race."

4. Express gratitude: "I'm thankful our
   school has this race every year since I
   love running."

WHAT ARE YOU PROUD OF?

Think about what you're proud of when it comes to what you've done in your life and what you like about yourself.

Don't hold back! Maybe you're proud of reading a long book or being a loyal friend. Maybe you're proud of doing something scary like performing in a talent show. Think of challenges you've overcome, hard decisions you've made, goals you've reached, and any accomplishments that are important to you.

These proud moments are great to go back and read about when you're a having a rough day and not feeling great about yourself. (We all have those days!)

PRESENT YOURSELF WITH AN AWARD.

Fill in the certificate with something you're proud of — and be creative but realistic: "Best Milkshake Maker in the Family!"

THIS CERTIFICATE BELONGS TO:

_____

FOR EXCELLENCE IN:

_____

_____

PROUD POSE!

. . . .

No matter where people
live around the world or
what culture they are a
part of, when people feel
proud, they have the same
body language: They tilt
their heads up and stand
straighter. If you need a
little extra courage, think of
something that makes you
proud and take this stance.

ASK LOVED ONES WHY THEY'RE PROUD OF YOU.

In Your Head
Coping Tool

You might be surprised by what you find out! Write down their answers here so you can remember all the positive ways others see you. You can use these positives (as well as the list of what you're proud of, on page 118) as a coping tool to balance out negative thoughts.

STEPS FOR HOW TO TAKE A COMPLIMENT

· · · · · · · · · · · · · ·

When someone tells you you're good at something or they like something about you, a lot of people have a hard time accepting the compliment. Kids may say, "I'm not that good" or disagree with the compliment in some way. If this sounds like you, practice how to take a compliment with two steps:

1. Say "Thank you."

2. Stop yourself from giving reasons the person shouldn't be proud of you, such as "it wasn't that hard" or "anyone could have done it." (Zip your lips if these words try to escape!)

WRITE ABOUT THE STEPS YOU TOOK TO REACH AN IMPORTANT GOAL.

If you win first place at a competition or earn the highest grade you've ever gotten on a test, it's easy to focus on the shiny gold medal or big "A+" to show your adults. But you can keep going to achieve more if you don't get too caught up in the final outcome. Think about an important goal you've accomplished, and write about all the steps you took to get there.

Focus on all the hard work you put in and how much you enjoyed the process — pride in your effort is what builds confidence and self-esteem more than the final outcome.

....

....

....

....

....

....

....

....

FEELING PROUD

· · · · · · · · · · · · · · · ·

Pride triggers the hormone dopamine, which is the feel-good chemical in the brain and body. When you're learning something new, the dopamine from feeling proud while you learn helps you work harder!

CHAPTER 9
GRATITUDE

FEELING THANKFUL...

...and appreciating what you have — that's what gratitude is all about.

Maybe you've said what you're grateful for at the Thanksgiving table, or you've written thank-you notes for birthday presents. These are common ways to think about and express gratitude — but the more gratitude you have, the better. In fact, scientists know that the more gratitude people feel, the happier and healthier they are overall, and the more resilient they are when times are tough.

Gratitude is special: it is considered an emotion and also a coping strategy, but it does not pop up in our brains and bodies automatically. It can take more effort to feel gratitude. This is because human brains focus on negatives much more easily than positives. The good news is that practicing activities that make you feel gratitude can actually change your brain, making it easier to notice the positives. Practice, practice, practice, because remembering what you're grateful for even when you're stressed, sad, and angry can help change your thinking and mood.

ANIMALS TOO!

Scientists have even seen animals show gratitude— from fish, birds, and bats to chimpanzees! They do helpful things for one another even if there might be a risk of getting hurt. In turn, the animals who were helped do nice things for the helpers later on.

GROW YOUR GRATITUDE GARDEN.

Take a few minutes to think about everything and everyone in your life you feel grateful for, and write each one in a flower in the garden.

DRAW MORE FLOWERS IF YOU HAVE MORE TO BE GRATEFUL FOR!

PAUSE FOR A TWO-MINUTE GRATITUDE MEDITATION.

Here's how to do it: Set a timer for one or two minutes and close your eyes. Think of everything you're grateful for today from the moment you woke up. When the timer goes off, write or draw what popped into your head during the meditation.

How do you feel after your gratitude meditation?

SAVE THIS SPACE FOR WHEN YOU'RE HAVING A HARD DAY.

Expression
Coping Tool

When it feels like everything is going wrong, challenge yourself to find some gratitude. Write here about what's making this a tough day and what you're still grateful for. Notice how you feel afterward!

....

....

....

....

....

....

....

....

....

WRITE A WHAT-IF STORY.

In Your Head
Coping Tool

Think of a big, positive event in your life — like meeting someone special to you, adopting a pet, or starting a new hobby. Now, write a story about how your life would be different if this event never happened.

Use your imagination to think about all that could have gone differently.

....

....

....

....

....

....

....

....

....

....

....

....

....

....

....

....

....

....

....

....

....

Thinking through these what-ifs helps us feel even more gratitude for the positive events and people in their lives.

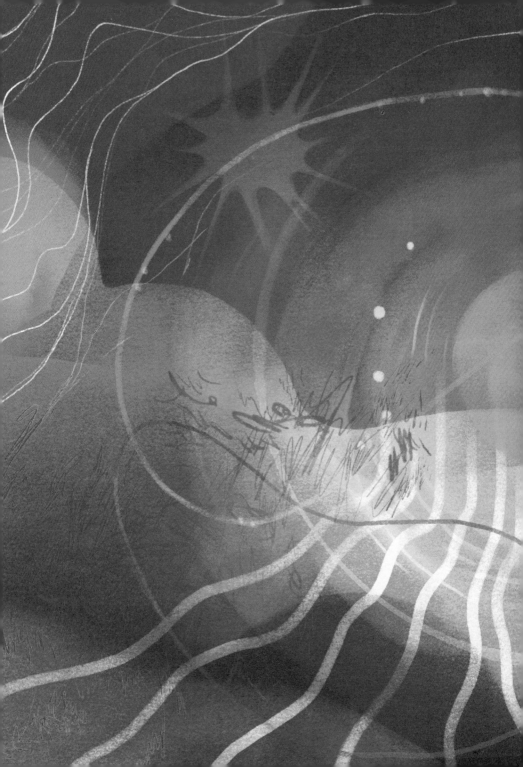

CHAPTER 10
ALLLLLLLLL THE FEELS!

CONGRATULATIONS!

You've almost reached the end. Hopefully, you've learned a few things about yourself and your feelings, including how to cope with tough emotions like anger and sadness, and how to embrace pleasant emotions like happiness and gratitude. Even though this journal covered some of the most common emotions, there are hundreds more — but you can use what you learned in these pages for any emotion that comes up.

IN THESE LAST PAGES, THINK ABOUT WHAT YOU GOT OUT OF KEEPING THIS JOURNAL.

QUESTIONS TO THINK ABOUT OR WRITE ABOUT:

1. What did I learn about myself?

2. What are my most common emotions?

3. Which emotions do I feel the most confident coping with, and which ones are harder for me to deal with?

4. How does my body react to emotions?

WRITE A LETTER TO YOURSELF IN FIVE YEARS.

How old will you be five years from now? What do you want to remind your future self about when it comes to coping with your emotions?

....

....

....

....

....

....

....

....

....

WHAT ADULT CAN BEST UNDERSTAND AND HELP YOU?

What do you want the most important adult in your life to know? Prepare a way to express your thoughts to them — either through sharing parts of this journal, writing them a note, or just telling them while spending time together.

WHAT I WANT .... TO KNOW:

....

....

....

....

HOW I WILL TELL THEM:

....

....

....

....

WHAT'S IN YOUR PERSONAL COPING TOOLBOX?

Look back through the journal and star your favorite coping strategies. How many fall into each category?

IN YOUR BODY

....

....

IN YOUR HEAD

....

....

EXPRESSION

....

....

CONNECTION

....

....

Now you know what works best for you! But as you grow and change, the coping that works best might too, so come back and keep updating this list.

EMOTIONS GLOSSARY

Have you ever felt like you have a lot of emotions at once? You could be feeling happy, confident, and proud all at the same time. Use this emotions glossary to add variety to your feelings vocabulary or to help you fill in the emotions stop on the Feelings Pathways. When you ask yourself, "how am I feeling?" you can have several answers!

LOVING
JOYFUL
CHEERFUL
CONTENT
GRATEFUL

ANGRY
IRRITABLE
ANNOYED
FRUSTRATED
JEALOUS

PROUD
CONFIDENT
OPTIMISTIC
HOPEFUL

SADNESS
HURT
MISERABLE
GRIEF

SHAMEFUL
GUILT
REGRET
LONELY

HAPPY
EXCITED
ENTHUSIASTIC
RELIEF
SURPRISED
AMAZED

WORRIED
SCARED
NERVOUS
ANXIOUS
EMBARRASSED

The information in this book is not meant to take the place of the
advice of your doctor or other medical practitioners.

Cover and book design by Caroline Pickering

Illustrations on cover and pages 6-7, 24-25, 38-39, 52-53, 66-67,
80-81, 94-95, 104-105, 114-115, 126-127, 136-137
by Cate Andrews
All other illustrations from Getty Images and Adobe Stock

Library of Congress Cataloging-in-Publication Data
available on request

10 9 8 7 6 5 4 3 2 1

Published by Hearst Home Kids, an imprint of
Hearst Books/Hearst Communications, Inc.
300 W 57th Street
New York, NY 10019

Hearst Home Kids, the Hearst Home Kids logo, and Hearst Books
are registered trademarks of Hearst Communications, Inc.

For information about custom editions, special sales, premium
and corporate purchases:
hearst.com/magazines/hearst-books

Printed in China
ISBN 978-1-950785-93-3